Contents

p20

p12

p34

p53

p75

p84

p112

Printed and Published in Great Britain by D. C. THOMSON & CO., LTD.,
185 Fleet Street, London EC4A 2HS
© D.C. THOMSON & CO., LTD., 2003.
While every reasonable care will be taken, neither D. C. Thomson & Co., Ltd., nor its agents accept any liability for loss or damage to colour transparencies or any other material submitted to this publication.

ISBN 0 85116 8264

Penny's Place

PENNY JORDAN'S parents owned two cafés, "Penny's Place" and "Penny's", a posh new café next door. Penny and her mates, Arlene, Gemma, Sita and Donna, were in "Penny's Place" talking about Christmas —

I don't know what's going to happen this year, Penny. Pete wants to go and live with Dad and Mum's in a mood about it!

Why, Arlene? What's the problem?

It's not like Pete to make a fuss.

No. But he doesn't like Mum's new boyfriend. I think Andy's cool — and Mum's been a different person since she met him.

Huh! I wish *my* ma and pa would have a change of character.

Anyway, must go. I said I'd meet Mum and help her choose a new top for her date tomorrow. See ya!

Yeah! 'Bye!

Oh, well, I'll have my usual Christmas, no doubt. One day off, then back to work in 'Penny's Place'! What about you, Donna?

The usual, too! The kids screaming and the adults fighting! Arlene's *lucky!*

5

Meanwhile —

Hey, that looks like Andy!

It *is* Andy! And he looks dead friendly with that woman.

Er, hi, Arlene. Out shopping, are you?

Hi, Andy. Yes. I'm going to meet Mum.

I'll see you, Arlene. We-we've got to go.

What's he up to? He looks dead embarrassed. Should I tell Mum, or what?

Arlene just couldn't decide.

What do you think, Arlene? Would this suit me?

What? Oh, I . . .

Is anything the matter, love? You look miles away.

No. I-I'm fine, Mum.

I can't tell her what I saw. If Andy was with another woman Mum'd be so hurt.

That evening Andy came over —

Sorry I didn't introduce you to Jen this afternoon, Arlene. She's a business associate and we were a bit busy.

Huh! And a bit too friendly for work colleagues. Is Pete right? Is Andy not to be trusted?

6

Next day, in "Penny's Place" —

Oh, Arlene. I hope Andy isn't cheating on your mum.

He *might* be telling the truth. Some business people can be really off-hand when they're busy.

Just then —

Anyone fancy coming with me to look at a new horse?

Yeah? You bet, Gemma.

Sounds cool. It'll take my mind off Andy.

So —

Why do you need a new horse, Gemma? Is Firefly too old?

No, but I need a bigger horse to enter more advanced competitions. Firefly can't manage anything too difficult.

But —

Yes, of course, Andy. I'll see you tonight at seven then.

That's the woman I saw talking to Andy — and it sounds like she's arranging to see him again. What's she doing here?

Riding for disabled children

She's Marianne Harper. She owns the stables, Arlene.

Arlene made an excuse to stay in the car —

Huh! Andy said her name was Jen. And she obviously *isn't* a business associate. Andy's work doesn't have anything to do with horses.

When Arlene arrived home —

Hi, Mum. Not getting ready for your date?

Andy had to go out of town at the last minute. We're meeting tomorrow, instead.

7

8

It'll cheer her up even more when you tell her that the woman was so mad she tipped her whole plate of pasta over Andy. Tomato sauce and all!

Ha, ha, ha! I wish I'd seen it! Wasn't *your* mum mad?

Nah! She said he'd asked for it. MInd you, it was me who had to tidy up!

Typical. It's always the kids who have to do the dirty work.

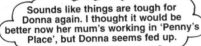

Sounds like things are tough for Donna again. I thought it would be better now her mum's working in 'Penny's Place', but Donna seems fed up.

And Gemma wasn't happy either. After school —

Now I've a new horse Mum and Dad want to sell Firefly. I — I never thought that would happen.

If I had the money I'd buy him. But I couldn't afford a *clothes* horse!

The hardest part is finding him a good home. I couldn't bear him going somewhere they didn't love him.

Later —

There's an advert here for the disabled riding school at the stables. I wonder if they need any new horses. Firefly would be great with kids.

So —

Yes, I'm always interested in looking at new horses for the school. Would your friend like me to come over?

I'll have to check. I'll get back to you.

And soon —

Yes, I'd like to buy Firefly, Gemma. He's just the steady friendly type of horse we need. And you can come and see him any time you like.

That'd be great, thanks.

And I'm sorry about what happened with your friend's mother, Penny. I had no idea Andy was seeing her as well. But now we've *both* split with the rat!

Huh! That's exactly what he deserves.

I know my mum and dad are hard up, Penny, but at least they're still together. And happy *most* of the time!

Yeah! I know what you mean, Donna.

But things were about to change for the Greens—

Guess what! My lottery numbers have come up!

Cool! Can we buy a new house? Or a boat, or . . .

No, Sharon. It's not *that* big a win. But it means I can pay off our debts and make a fresh start. But not a word to Pa. I plan to surprise him — in a *big* way!

Continued on page 65

EYES DOWN!

Can you find the names of twenty four animals hidden in our wordsearch? Names can read up, down, back, forwards or diagonally, and letters can be used more than once. When you have found everything, unscramble the remaining letters to spell out the name of *another* animal. What is it? Have fun! *Solution on page 119.*

```
S E L E P H A N T S E C
R U A Y L B G G O D E H
K K M I E I E R D R Z E
H A O A R K E A L A N E
O N N A T C N L R Z A T
R T F G O O A O R I P A
S F A N A M P M D L M H
E V I C A R P O E A I G
A H Y N O P O E P L H O
R E T S M A H O E P C A
C O W M O N K E Y H I T
T I G E R E S U O M S H
```

Bear	Elephant	Lizard
Camel	Giraffe	Llama
Cat	Goat	Monkey
Cheetah	Hamster	Mouse
Chimpanzee	Hippopotamus	Pony
Cow	Horse	Rhinoceros
Dog	Kangaroo	Sheep
Donkey	Lion	Tiger

in colour!

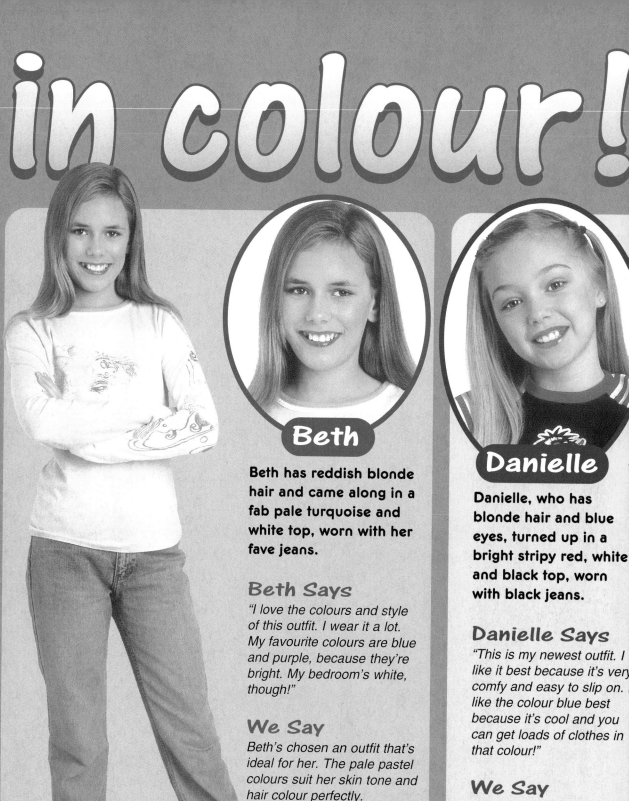

Beth

Beth has reddish blonde hair and came along in a fab pale turquoise and white top, worn with her fave jeans.

Beth Says

"I love the colours and style of this outfit. I wear it a lot. My favourite colours are blue and purple, because they're bright. My bedroom's white, though!"

We Say

Beth's chosen an outfit that's ideal for her. The pale pastel colours suit her skin tone and hair colour perfectly.

See pages 40 + 41 for more colour choices for Beth.

Danielle

Danielle, who has blonde hair and blue eyes, turned up in a bright stripy red, white and black top, worn with black jeans.

Danielle Says

"This is my newest outfit. I like it best because it's very comfy and easy to slip on. I like the colour blue best because it's cool and you can get loads of clothes in that colour!"

We Say

Red and black are both dramatic colours which really suit blondes, and it's an easy, comfy outfit to wear. Top marks!

Check out pages 82 + 83 for more colour tips for Danielle.

Meet Beth, Danielle and Hannah - three girls with different colouring and looks!

Miss-Chievous

Hannah

Hannah chose a cool hippy look, with her favourite appliquéd jeans and a brown strappy top. She'd added a chain belt, bracelet and thong necklace, too.

Hannah Says

"I like these colours a lot and I think everything goes together really well. I think pink and blue are really nice colours, too. I wear a lot of blue clothes, but my bedroom's done in purple and lilac."

We Say

Brown doesn't always suit brunettes, but Hannah's choice is spot on! Her accessories finish off the look perfectly!

Discover more cool colours for Hannah on pages 106 + 107.

13

Are you starry-eyed?

Find out with this fun quiz!

START

Do you always read your stars?

Y / N

Has your horoscope ever come true?

Do you read more than one horoscope a day?

Do you believe in luck?

Y / N

N

You'd worry if your stars were 'bad'. True?

Would you like to visit a fortune teller?

Do you think you're typical of your star sign?

Y / N

Y

Y / N

Do you have a lucky number?

Are your stars the first thing you look at in a magazine?

You only believe your stars when they're 'good'. True?

Do you think horoscopes are just made up?

Y / N

Y / N

N / Y

N / Y

You love reading your stars and you wouldn't dream of doing something if your stars advised against it. But beware! This could lead to you missing out on all kinds of adventures!

Sometimes you read your stars, sometimes you don't. You're usually too busy to pay them much attention. You don't take them very seriously, but don't mind if other people do.

Do you believe in the stars? Pah! You think horoscopes are rubbish and don't mind saying so! But try not to be too critical. Lots of people do enjoy reading them. So why not take a peek?

Let's Pretend!

Joanne had fancied Mark for ages —

Hi, Joanne. Did you see that new comedy programme last night?

Er — no, Mark.

Did *you* see it, Lynn?

No, sorry, Mark. What was it about?

Tch! Why couldn't *I* have said that? Lynn's dead confident. Every time *I* see Mark, I just clam up.

Back home —

It's because I like Mark so much that I feel so awkward talking to him.

Hey, what's this . . . ? 'My throat went dry as soon as I saw Dave, so I practised talking to someone who wasn't so important to me.'

That's what I'll do! I'll practise chatting to someone I *don't* fancy. Then I can pretend I'm chatting to them when I'm talking to Mark.

And later, in town —

There's Simon. I like him a lot — but I don't fancy him. He'll be ideal to practise on.

So —

Hi, Simon. I — I like your trainers.

Thanks, Jo. They're from the new sports shop.

16

Really? I might take a look later.

You should. They've got a great selection.

Ten minutes later —

That was easy. I was nice and relaxed, because I wasn't trying to impress him.

Joanne took every chance to speak to Simon —

. . . and then old Granger said we needed a break. I couldn't believe it!

Ha, ha, ha! No wonder, Joanne!

I really enjoy talking to you, Jo. You're dead chatty and interesting.

Oh! I — er — thanks, Simon.

It's working. I'm *definitely* more confident now.

So, at the youth club —

There's Mark — looking gorgeous as usual. All I have to do is pretend he's Simon, and it should be easy to talk to him.

Hi, Mark. How are you?

Fine, Jo. I was just telling Paul about the holiday Mum and Dad have booked for us to Portugal.

Where about? We were in the Algarve last year and it was great.

Cool! Could you let me see some photographs?

17

Let's visit... FRANCE

Paris

Lots to see and do in the capital city. Climb aboard an open-topped bus and whizz around all the top city sights. Then take a boat trip on the Seine, have a picnic and feed the birds in the Tuileries Gardens, stop for a coffee (or a McDonalds) on the Champs Elysees and then shop till you drop. Finally, go to the top of the Eiffel Tower for one of the best city views in the world. Phew!

Disneyland Paris

Well worth a visit – in fact, well worth a holiday. Disneyland is easy to reach and, once you're there, it's non-stop fun with Mickey and his mates.

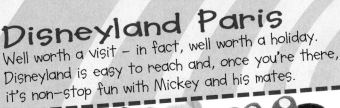

It's a riot!

Wot an eyeful!

Beaches

With the English Channel, the Atlantic Ocean and the Mediterranean Sea all lapping its shores, France has loadsa fabby beaches. The Med may be the warmest, but the Atlantic Coast has probably the best sands of all.

Cannes

In the sunny South of France, Cannes used to be a sleepy little fishing village. Now it's where to go to do some star gazing – especially during the Cannes International Film Festival in May. Then the streets are **crammed** with stars.

You never know WHO you might bump into at Cannes

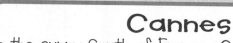

Food

French food has been famed for years - and no wonder. Cheese, bread, pate and fruit make ideal picnic nosh, and crepes or French fries are yummy at any time. However, we're not so sure about snails, frogs' legs and horse meat. Mmm!

A perfect French style picnic.

French Fancies

No, not the sweet little iced cakes, but things that make France famous.

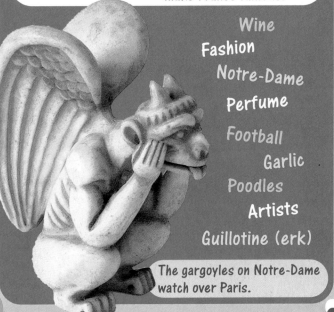

Wine
Fashion
Notre-Dame
Perfume
Football
Garlic
Poodles
Artists
Guillotine (erk)

The gargoyles on Notre-Dame watch over Paris.

Quick Quiz

(Answers on page 119)

Which of these is NOT a city in France?

Paris
Nancy
Brittany
Lourdes

Who was Quasimodo?

What is the French name for a castle?

Did You Know?

* Calais is less than 40km from England.
* France is bordered by six countries; Belgium, Luxembourg, Germany, Switzerland, Italy and Spain.
* 'Je ne comprends pas' means 'I do not understand' in French. 'Parlez-vous anglais?' is 'Do you speak English?'.

Use Your Loaf

Bread recipes from around the world

FRENCH TOAST
You might call it eggy bread, but its real name is French Toast. And here's how to make the perfect plateful.

Ingredients:
2 slices of bread
1 egg
Half a cupful of milk
Seasoning to taste
Oil for frying

Method:
Beat the egg and milk together and season to taste. Trim the crusts from each slice of bread and then dip them in the beaten egg, making sure all parts of the bread are coated. Heat the oil and fry each slice until golden brown.

French Toast is delicious served with bacon or beans - or for something really special, dust each slice with a little icing sugar.

Always ask an adult's permission before using kitchen equipment.

it's Christmas!

2 pages packed with festive fun, so get puzzlin'.
Answers are on page 119 - but no peepin'!

Scrambled!

Fit the tiles into the grid to spell out a message. We've put a few in place to start you off.

	PY		IDA			
MA				L R		ERS

AN	MA	TO	PY	HAP	HOL	L R
IDA	ERS	NDY	ALL	YS	EAD	NUA

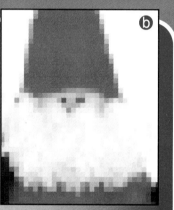

ⓐ

ⓑ

ⓒ

ⓓ

The Name Game

These people all have names which are associated with Christmas. Can you recognise them? (Okay, one is a bit of a cheat, but it does sound Christmassy.)

Go Glitter!

Solve the clues, then unscramble the letters in the shaded squares to find something to do with Christmas.

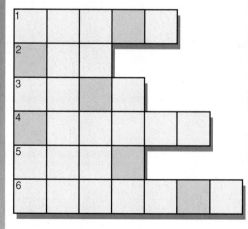

1. They ring
2. A climbing plant
3. Decorate this
4. Eaten at Christmas
5. Tie these on gifts
6. Figgy or plum?

22

Hang Around!

Solve the clues in our mini crossie! It's as simple as that!

Across:
2. Late night visitor.
3. White rain.
6. Main meal.

Down:
1. Wrap these at Christmas.
2. Hang this up on Christmas Eve.
4. A fun play - like Cinderella.
5. Send these in the post.

Odd One Out!

Rudolph's four cousins have come to stay with him. The cousins are identical - but Rudolph is slightly different. Can you spot him?

START ▶

W/S
G J A

Puzzling!

Find your way through the maze to the gift, then unscramble the letters to discover what's inside.

JULIE Rutter gazed at the box, wonderment on her face. It was the most beautiful box she'd ever seen, its carved mahogany walls inlaid with the most striking jewels of blue and green. Carefully, she lifted its lid. Inside was a nest of midnight blue velvet, waiting to welcome Julie's most special treasures.

She glanced up at the stall keeper – it was old Miss Turvey. Miss Turvey was quite well off, so the box was probably as valuable as it looked. But the price on the lid was only five pounds. Julie had exactly that amount in her pocket.

The young girl bit her lip. That money was all she had left to buy Gran Rutter a Christmas present. Julie had really set out for the village sweet shop where she meant to buy a small box of her gran's favourite continental chocolates. The chocolates came in several different box sizes, but were so expensive, Julie could only afford the smallest. But if Julie bought Miss Turvey's jewellery box for herself, there'd be nothing left for Gran.

Julie, one hand on the box, agonised over what to do. In the corner of her eye, she saw Melissa Morris straining to see what she was doing. Julie's eyes narrowed. Trust Melissa Morris to turn up. Julie was sick of Melissa following her around all the

time. She was nosy and a sneak, and nobody in the village liked her.

Just then, Melissa spied the box and Julie saw the look of interest on her face. "Hey," she shouted, rudely elbowing her way to the front of the crowd. "How much is that box?"

Miss Turvey answered, "Five pounds."

"I'll take it!" Julie squeaked, hurriedly. Before she quite knew what she was doing, Julie had pressed the money into Miss Turvey's hand, and was hurrying away,

hugging the precious box and relishing the look of anger on Melissa's face.

It was only when she stepped out of the church hall and into the snow, that she realised she'd made a big mistake.

A small drawer slid out

Back in her room, Julie slowly turned the box in her hands, and ached with guilt. It was beautiful beyond words and she desperately wanted to keep it. But now, because of her jealousy and

Box

selfishness, Julie had no money left to buy a present for Gran Rutter.

Perhaps she could give the box to Gran for Christmas. But Gran had plenty of jewellery boxes and wouldn't want another. Perhaps she could ask Miss Turvey to buy it back. Perhaps she could ask Melissa if she would like to … but, no – that would be too horrible!

As she toyed with the box, she suddenly heard a sharp twanging noise, and a small drawer slid out from the bottom.

"A secret compartment!" Julie gasped.

But what was hidden inside the compartment truly took her breath away - a beautiful brooch, solid gold and inset with glittering amber, lay on the midnight blue velvet. Carefully, Julie lifted it out and turned it under the light. The brooch was heavy and looked expensive, and Julie knew immediately that its frame and stones were real.

"Miss Turvey must be out of her mind with worry searching for this," she whispered to herself.

For a moment, Julie thought about keeping the brooch, but then shook her head. She'd been selfish enough, and she couldn't do a thing like that to an old woman – especially so near to Christmas time. With a sigh, she pulled on her coat.

"It was my mother's"

Miss Turvey was at home when Julie found her. She gazed at the brooch and shook her head.

"I-I've looked everywhere for this," she said quietly. "It was my mother's and I thought I'd never see it again!"

"It looks very expensive," Julie replied, thrilling at the delight on the old woman's face.

"It's worth several hundred pounds," Miss Turvey told her as Julie's jaw dropped in amazement. "But it's worth a lot more than that to me."

Miss Turvey placed the brooch carefully on the table and rummaged in her handbag. "I must give you something," she said, pulling out her purse. But Julie held up her hand and shook her head. She'd already been too greedy, and didn't want to make matters worse.

"No, Miss Turvey. It's yours, and I don't want anything for returning it to you," she insisted.

"But I can't let such honesty go unrewarded," Miss Turvey replied.

Julie backed towards

the door, shaking her head. She thought about Gran Rutter. About the present she should have bought for her. She knew now what she had to do. She must confess to Mum, and ask her to lend her some more money.

Feeling brighter, she pushed open the door and stepped into the snow.

"But it's Christmas," Miss Turvey insisted, following her into the cold. "And you've made it such a happy one for me."

"I don't want your money, Miss Turvey," Julie insisted, face reddening with embarrassment.

"Well, at least take this." Miss Turvey reached into her porch, and thrust a gold- coloured box into Julie's hand. Julie stared at the box, and her eyes widened with disbelief. It was the biggest box of chocolates Julie had ever seen – Gran Rutter's favourite continental chocolates.

"Thank you, Miss Turvey," she gasped, hugging the old woman with delight. "It's going to be a happy Christmas for everyone!"

"I remember the day I first met her —"

You ain't staying here! No rent — no room, that's my motto! Out you go!

Please, Mrs Patterson. I beg of you.

Don't cry, you poor boy. I will help you.

Wh-who are you?

They call me Miss Angel. And you?

I'm Master Peter Hewitt, late of Belgravia Square.

That's a rich part of town! What has brought you from a wealthy home to a back-street lodging house?

Ill fortune. A few months ago my father died. Up until then, we had lived in grandeur.

But on my father's death, my mama discovered that in reality we were deeply in debt. The house was sold to pay our creditors, and Mama and I moved into Mrs Patterson's lodging house.

Mama took a job in a match factory. But then God took my mama away from me, too. The factory burned down . . .

I remember that. There were no proper fire exits, so the workers inside didn't stand a chance. Poor lad, to lose his mother in such tragic circumstances.

28

Thank you for your offer — but I reject it. Good day, Miss Angel.

No! Peter! Come back!

My illness has weakened me. I cannot run after him.

Don't upset yourself, Miss Angel. I heard him — the toffee-nosed fool! If he don't want your help, you can't force him, can you? He didn't deserve it, anyway.

Don't be hard on him, Annie. He has been brought up to expect the best. It must be difficult for him to adapt. But I must seek him out and try to persuade him to change his mind.

"So Miss Angel searched the streets for me, night after night, until —"

Peter! So there you are!

Sleeping under a railway arch! Surely he will come to the stable house now. It is a palace compared to this.

"But I was too proud —"

No! I cannot come! To move into a stable would be admitting defeat. I shall not leave here until I have a *proper* home to go to. I will find one soon. Don't worry!

But I *do* worry! I cannot help it. Peter has no friends, and he looks even thinner and weaker now. He will die on these mean streets — and all because his stupid pride will not let him live in a stable.

It is a sad state of affairs — and at Christmas time, too. Of course! That's it! Christmas!

"The following day —"

If you will not come and live with us, at least let me give you some food, Peter.

Thank you, Miss Angel. I will repay you one day.

I do not ask for any repayment, but if you wish to help me, you can do it now. My arms are weary. Would you carry my basket?

Of course I will, Miss Angel.

The poor boy is so thin and weak, he will find it hard to carry the basket. But I need him to come with me for my plan to succeed.

"Miss Angel visited several shops, then —"

Let us stop off at the church and say a Christmas prayer.

Oh, yes! Mama taught me how to pray, Miss Angel.

Cat Deeley

Pressies For Pets

Not all presents for your pet cat or dog need to be expensive - here are a few ideas for things that will amuse your pet for hours - and some of them are probably already in your house!

CATS

Bounce a ping pong ball along the floor and watch the fun. Cats love the way it makes a noise hitting off walls - and it's light enough for them to push around with their paws.

A feather toy is easy to make. You'll need a stick like a cane, a few feathers, a bit of thick wool and a little bell, if possible. Cut a length of wool approximately 30cm long. Attach the wool to one end of the stick by winding thread round and round it, so that the wool is now hanging down. Tie a few feathers to the other end of the wool, using thread again. If you have a small bell (like the ones on a cat collar), secure it to the end

of the stick where the wool is tied. When you dangle the feathers towards your cat, the bell will catch its attention, too!

Plant catmint in the garden. Catmint can be bought at your nearest garden centre and once the plant has grown, you'll see your cat rolling about on it and generally behaving in a very odd way! Cats just *love* it! You can pick some and put it inside a piece of material. Sew up all the sides and give it to your cat to play with.

Play games with a torch or small mirror. Cats love to chase reflections, so you can use a mirror to reflect

PET SHOP BUYS

If you want to **buy** a pressie for your cat or dog, here are some ideas.

Pussy pressies

Wobbling toy £2.99. Paw-powered fun toy!

Trailing toy £3.99. This snake-like toy will have your cat chasing it for hours!

Catnip treats £1.99. See your cat go wild for these tasty treats!

KOOKAMUNGA CATNIP TREATS
SALMON FLAVORED
Pure Frantic Fun
NET WT 5 OZ (141 g)

Cat place mat £1.49. No more spills on Mum's clean floor!

I ♥ CATS

Catnip bag £1.19. Watch your cat purr and play at the same time!

toy will be even more fun if it has a noise coming from it! If you have a squeaker or a little bell, you can sew that inside.

A deflated football - your dog can get a good grip of a ball with no air in it. That can be better fun for the dog as he can shake it about as he runs around with it!

sunshine in a room. You can get the same effect by shining a small torch in a dark room. The faster you move the beam of light, the more fun your cat will have!

DOGS

Play tug-of-war with a short length of rope that has a knot at each end. Your dog will love to tug at the knot at his end and the other knot will give you something to hold on to!

A bone is good for your dog's teeth, so if your mum or gran makes soup using a bone, once the bone is cool, you can let your dog chew on it. But never give your dog chicken or turkey bones! They are very brittle and can be dangerous if eaten.

A toy to play with - you can make one out of lots of old socks or tights sewn up inside another old sock. The ball-like

Doggy pressies

Squeaky newpaper toy £1.99. For the dog who likes to fetch the paper!

Safari bone £1.99. A soft squeaky toy that will drive you mad!

Dental chew £3.59. It's chicken flavoured and good for teeth!

Dog place mat £1.49. Avoid messy dog food on the floor!

Lost in the Mist

38

Brown Bears

*Brown bears aren't always brown. They can also be black, blond or red.

*During the winter, bears grow an extra layer of fat and fur to keep them warm. Then, when the warmer (hopefully) weather comes, they shed it again. A bit like us putting on our winter clothes, really.

*Bears are expert fishers and climbers, so don't try to hide from one by climbing a tree – or disguising yourself as a fish!

*A fully grown brown bear can be as much as 3.5 metres tall (gulp!) and can weigh - wait for it – over 600 kilos! Erk!

*Food isn't a big problem, as bears will eat almost anything they can get their paws on. Nuts, fruits, fish – even insects.

*Bears sometimes wake up during hibernation. When they do, they usually go searching for food.

in colour!

Beth's warm colouring - reddish blonde hair and greyish blue eyes - means she can wear bright and delicate colours, but looks best in natural tones.

Beth's first look was this floaty lace top and cream trousers. We kept Beth's make up nice and natural with neutral shades of cream and brown. Beth was delighted.
"I love this top - I'm going to ask my mum to buy it for me."

*Colours to try if *you* have similar colouring, are green, turquoise, white and purple.
**Warm* browns and cream can look fantastic, too.
*Colours to *keep away from* are reds and pinks as they can clash with your colouring.
* You suit both black and white. Lucky you!

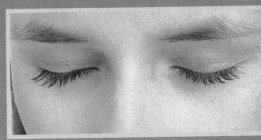

Next we tried more dramatic colours to show Beth that she doesn't always have to stick to neutrals. Her bright turquoise top and lilac trousers looked fab! A little purple and pink eyeshadow and Beth was well impressed.

"I never usually wear make up, but I really like what I'm wearing today," she said happily.

*Reddish hair suits natural wooden clasps and other accessories.
*It can also be beautifully wild and wavy.
*Bronze or copper jewellery suit you better than silver or gold. Wear clothes in these colours, too, to emphasise your delicate colouring.

Let's visit... SWITZERLAND

Travel on a tram for a great view of the Matterhorn.

Climate

With all that snow, we tend to think of Switzerland as a very cold country, but the average summer temperature in Zurich is warmer than in London. Winters are a bit colder, though, so you'll need to pack your woollies.

Heidi

Aaaaw! Almost everyone knows the story of Heidi, the little orphan sent to live with her grandfather in the Swiss mountains. If not, pop to your local library or bookshop and grab a copy. It's soooo good! Everybody say...'aaaaw'.

HEIDI
BY
JOHANNA SPYRI

Priory Classics

Mountains

Think Switzerland and you immediately think of mountains – and probably the most famous Swiss mountain of all is the Matterhorn. Its pointed shape looks just like a piece of Toblerone – but it probably doesn't taste as good.

Boats

Although Switzerland is a land-locked country and, therefore, has no beaches, there are lots of lakes. Don't miss out on a summer boat trip. Cruising on Lake Geneva is one of the nicest ways to spend a sunny day.

Quick Quiz
(Answers on page 119)

Which is the odd one out?

Basel

Bellinzona

Belladonna

Bern

Who famously shot an apple off his son's head?

How do you make a Swiss Roll?

Swish Swiss

What makes Switzerland smile.

Cheese

Fondue

Skiing

Chocolate

Banks

Cuckoo Clocks

Watches

Yodelling

William Tell

Swiss Rolls

(We know they're not really Swiss but we think they're swish!)

Mmmmm! A chocolate dream!

Did You Know?

* There are four official languages in Switzerland.

* The Swiss Guard isn't found in Switzerland. The soldiers actually guard the Pope in the Vatican City in Rome.

* Switzerland is bordered by five countries; France, Italy, Austria, Germany and Liechtenstein.

Tennis

One of Switzerland's greatest ever sports personalities was tennis player Martina Hingis. Martina hit the top in 1997 and stayed there for four years. Unfortunately, injury hit the talented Swiss miss and she announced her retiral

Swiss Miss?

in February 2003 at the age of 22. One small problem, though, is that she was actually born in Slovakia and named after the famous Czech (now American) player, Martina Navratilova. Never mind, the Swiss loved her!

Use Your Loaf

Bread recipes from around the world

SWISS FONDUE FOR CHEATS

Real Swiss Fondue requires a fondue set and lots of expensive cheese and wine, but our cheat's version can be enjoyed by everyone. All you need is a good loaf of bread (or cake) cut into cubes (about 3cm), a fork for each person and a variety of dips. Melted cheese is a favourite - as is melted chocolate - but here are some other suggestions. Try them, or make your own. It's great fun!

SPICY TOMATO

Fry up half an onion (chopped) and one crushed clove of garlic gently in a little oil. Add a small tin of tomatoes and a pinch of chilli powder to taste. Cook together for ten minutes, then pass the mixture through a sieve, or blend to make a smooth dip for your bread cubes.

(Make sure the sauce isn't too hot before putting it in your mouth.)

SWEET DREAM

Chop or mash the fruit and juice from a tin of your favourite fruit. Add it to a tub of vanilla yoghurt and use cubes of cake to dip.

Always ask an adult's permission before using kitchen equipment.

Beauty and the Beast

Chloe Spenser was very popular with the other pupils at her school — both girls and boys! One day as she was coming out of the maths class —

That was tough going! Maths will never be my favourite subject.

Me neither, Chloe! Let's go and have a Coke at Luigi's before we go home.

Did you hear that, Rob? Chloe's going to be at the cafe after school. Think I'll just go along and 'accidentally' bump into her!

I think you're wasting your time, Steve. She's not interested.

Well, I'll make her interested. I want to ask her to a disco a week on Saturday.

Every boy in the class wants to ask Chloe out, including me!

And —

What do you think you're playing at, asking Chloe out? You knew Steve wanted to take her to the disco.

I don't know what you're talking about.

Yeah, you do. She told Rob she was out with you last night.

Some mate *he* turned out to be!

I don't know why he's denying it.

Just then —

I saw you in the park with Ben last night.

Yeah? He's a bit scruffy, but he's dead cute!

I'm going to the park again on Saturday. We'll probably watch a bit of the football match. Ben loves football!

Right — we'll catch them together and I'll have it out with him. You going to come along to give me some moral support?

Yes, okay.

49

happy families?

Do you love or hate your brothers and sisters? Is it better being older or younger than the others in your house? Here's what some readers think!

Barbara, 7, has a little brother, Joshua, aged 1½.

"I love my little brother. Sometimes I sing to him, and he gives me a huge smile and snuggles up to me. I wanted a little brother or sister for ages. I was so excited when Mum and Dad told me I was getting one.

When he arrived he was so cute, and he brought me a present that I'd always wanted – a huge painting kit! I couldn't believe it.

I get fed up when he keeps crying but Mum and Dad remind me that I'm still their favourite daughter. Joshua has just started copying things I say, like 'right then' and 'cool'. It sounds so sweet!"

Amanda, 8, has an older brother Jack, 10.

"I like having an older brother because I get to meet his friends, and we can do things together. At my grandma's seventieth birthday party we pretended to be pop stars. Everyone thought that was hilarious.

I go to an all girls' school, and Jack goes to an all boys' school, so when his class has parties I sometimes get invited. All my friends are really jealous that I have an older brother. I think some of them fancy him, too. Mum reckons I'm lucky as well, because she was one of five girls.

Sometimes Jack and I fight, though. He always grabs the TV remote control so that he can watch what he wants.

I also get fed up when he goes into my dad's office during the holidays to help out.

But then Jack complains that Mum buys me more new clothes than him!"

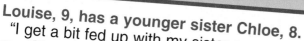

Louise, 9, has a younger sister Chloe, 8.

"I get a bit fed up with my sister sometimes, because she always wants to copy me. She looks a bit like me, because we've both got blonde curly hair, and sometimes people think we're twins.

I get mad when Mum and Dad let Chloe do what she wants. It took me ages to persuade them to let me join the Brownies, but once I'd joined Chloe was allowed to join at once. And they didn't like me using nail varnish, but when I got some as a present, Chloe was given some, too.

We have to share a room, so she's always borrowing my stuff. We have huge rows about it.

Sometimes, though, I do like having a sister. If we both nag Mum and Dad about the same thing, eventually they'll give in. Also, it's fun to do things like quizzes together. The other week, when she went to Brownie camp, I missed her - even although I had our bedroom to myself."

Jessica, 7, is an only child and doesn't like it.

"I don't really like being an only child - especially when we go on holiday. Mum and Dad don't really understand what I like doing, so we go around boring museums and galleries, while all my friends are probably on the beach. And, because I'm the only child on both sides of the family, we always have to visit old relatives who want to kiss me.

It also makes my parents really protective. There are so many things I'm not allowed to do - fireworks, funfairs and lots of other things are just too 'dangerous'.

Sometimes I feel left out of things. I'm sure if I had a brother or sister life would be a bit more interesting, and I keep asking Mum and Dad when I'm going to get one.

My friends from big families say I'm really lucky, as they have to share all their things, but I think it's boring being an only child. I keep hoping that one day I won't be one."

I used to love school. I was never top in exams, but I enjoyed almost every class. I got on quite well with the teachers, too - well, except Miss Drew in maths, and *nobody* got on with her! I had lots of friends and we joined loads of clubs and generally had fun. Yeah, life was pretty good back then. But everything changed when Dad got a new job down south.

To begin with he travelled down on a Sunday night and stayed in digs until Friday, when he came back home. That way Mum kept her job at the local hospital and I was able to stay on at my school. It seemed ideal. But after a few months we could see that Dad was exhausted and, to tell the truth, Mum and I missed him a lot during the week.

"I think we need to have a talk about moving," Mum said one day. "All this travelling is beginning to make your dad ill."

What Mum said was true and, while I didn't want to move, I knew we didn't really have a choice. Besides, I told myself, I could always keep in touch with

Bullies!
A reader tells her story

my old friends by phone or e-mail – and I'd soon make *new* friends, too. Hey, maybe it would be even *more* fun.

How wrong could I be? Oh, I loved our new house and I loved all the great shops. I even liked my new school - for the first week, anyway.

Pictures posed by models

The girls were quite friendly when I started, but gradually I noticed that they seemed to be avoiding me. When I came into a room, a few girls in my class began to snigger and whisper about me. Then, to make things worse, they began to mimic my accent and make fun of me. It was horrible.

I felt as if I didn't have a friend in the world. I tried to lose myself in my work, but then the bullies called me a swot and a teachers' pet! I knew I should report them, but I thought that would only make things worse so, instead, I just wandered off on my own and tried to block out all the nasty remarks and giggling.

I thought I was hiding things quite well, but it wasn't long before Mum noticed that something was wrong. Then, after a particularly awful day at school, I broke down and told her the whole story. She was horrified - and so was Dad when we told him later.

"There's no way you're going back there until this has been sorted out," he said. "We'll speak to the Head tomorrow and make sure this bullying stops."

And it did. Actually, it turned out that it was only a couple of girls who had been making things bad for me. The rest were just too scared to say anything in case the bullies started on them. The bullies had been warned before, so this time they were moved to another class - well away from me.

That all happened a year ago and I've made lots of new friends now. I still keep in touch with my old mates, though, and I make a special effort to be nice to any new girls who come to school. After all, I can remember how awful it was for *me*!

Giraffes

*A fully-grown male giraffe can measure around 5.5 metres. Just as well there aren't many bridges where they live!

*Female giraffes spend up to half of each day looking for food.
Typical – it's always the woman who has to do the shopping!

*Their long legs mean that giraffes are very good at kicking. Roll on the next World Cup!

*Some ancient Greeks and Egyptians thought giraffes were a cross between camels and leopards. As a result they came up with a weird and not very original name for them – cameleopards!

*Giraffes can weigh as much as a car. Now there's a useful fact – not!

*Giraffes have 45cm long, sticky tongues which are very useful for reaching food.

Meet the girls from BYKER GROVE

It's one of our favourite TV shows, so we popped along for a chat with some of the girlies from the latest series.
And there's more fun with the girls over on page 56.

SARAH

Real name: Sammy Dobson
Date of Birth: 27.11.86
Born: I was born in Ward 10 of Rake Lane Hospital, North Shields, at 18.36 on a wet and wintry Thursday.
Family: I'm an only child - but my dad is a bit of a kid at times, so he's kinda like a big brother.
Fave Toy: When I was small I had a trolley filled with coloured bricks, which I loved. I also had a huge stuffed tortoise called Tortie! My dad used to sit me on top and then fly me around on it.
Memories: I can remember my dad dressing up as a large rabbit. I thought it was a real big bunny at first, but soon realised who it was. I think that was on my second or third birthday.
Friends: I have loadsa 'best' friends - cos I think it's dangerous to have only one. I mean, if you fell out you wouldn't have **any** friends. Five of my friends are from school, one from my drama class and two from the cast of Byker Grove.

REGINA

Real name: Jade Turnbull
Date of Birth: 25.11.88
Born: Sunderland General Hospital
Family: Big brothers, Aidan and Dean.
Fave toy: I used to have a fluffy yellow duck - which I loved - but it went missing ages ago. I also went through a real

HAYLEY
Real name: Heather Kate Garrott
Date of Birth: 13.7.89
Born: Princess Mary Maternity Hospital in Newcastle.
Family: Big sister, Rosalyn.
Fave Toy: 'Doggy', a grey dog with a brown eye patch that my sister gave me. I still have him - and still love him!
Memories: My first memory was playing an angel in a Christmas play. I wore a white sheet and a tinsel crown. My friend, Suzy, wore a gold halo and I thought we were both brilliant.
Friends: I'm still best friends with Suzy, but some of my other friends are Ellie, Claire, Andrea, Alli, Lucy and Sam. I've also become good friends with Sammy (Sarah) and Nisha (Anjali) from Byker Grove.

LEANNE
Real name: Rachael Lee
Date of Birth: 2.3.87
Born: Shotley Bridge Hospital, Consett.
Family: I have two sisters and one brother. Steph, Hannah and Mattie. They're all younger than me.
Fave Toy: My favourite toy was a big doll. When I got her she was twice the size of me and I thought she was great. I don't know what happened to her, but I haven't seen her for years.
Memories: I was coming down a water slide on my dad's knee. He promised that I wouldn't go under the water - but, guess what! I did! I was really scared and made lots of noise.
Friends: I have lots and lots of good friends, but my best friends of all are Heather and Becky. We've been friends since we were five - and we're just as close now as we were then.

EVE
Real name: Rory Lewis
Date of Birth: 24.1.90
Born: I was born at UCH. (That's University College Hospital in London.)
Family: I've got one big sister, Nadia.
Fave Toy: When I was little I used to love my teddy bears very, very much. Unfortunately, I don't have any of them left now. (Awww!)
Memories: One of my earliest memories was getting lost in the snow. We were in America and I hadn't a clue where I was. I can't remember what age I was - but the memory is clear. It all ended happily though, but it was scary at the time.
Friends: My very best friend is Erin. She used to live across the road from me, but then she moved away. Now she lives in Stoke on Trent - but we're still friends.

ANJALI
Real name: Nisha Joshi
Date of Birth: 20.2.87
Born: I was born in Bishop Auckland General Hospital in County Durham.
Family: I have one sister, Sona, who is 28 years old.
Fave Toy: I was a bit of a tomboy when I was young and my favourite toy was my red toy train.
Memories: I was at nursery and it was time for dessert. I was given a banana pudding - but I screamed and screamed because I wanted a strawberry one. I think I was about one and a half at the time, so I suppose there was an excuse for my behaviour. I don't know if I ever did get the strawberry dessert, though.
Friends: I get on well with quite a few of the Byker Grove cast. One of my best mates is Ian, who is new. We first met at drama and have known each other for around five years. My best friend of all is my sister. We get on really well together - even although she is older. She lives in London, but we have lots of long girlie chats on the phone and I visit her often for real girlie weekends.

yoyo craze a few years back and, don't tell anyone, but I had a 'blanket' when I was younger.
Memories: The first thing I really remember was scooting around in my baby walker with my fluffy yellow duck held firmly by my side. Awwww!
Friends: Catherine lives four doors down from me and we've been 'bessies' ever since I can remember. My other really close friend is Sarah, who I met when I was in Year 7.

GROVE GOSS

* All the girls from Byker Grove (and the boys, too) come from ordinary schools, rather than full time stage schools. So, when they're not acting, they're doing the same things as you are.
* They think they're really lucky to be in Byker Grove and, although they get off school when they're filming, they have a tutor with them so they don't actually miss lessons. And acting is hard work, too, as there are always lines to learn and moves to remember – but the cast does get paid, so it's worthwhile.
* All the girls are in some kind of school or local drama group and that's where film and TV companies go when they are looking for children. So, if you fancy being a star, why not ask at your local theatre or library for details of drama groups in your area? You might end up on TV sooner than you think!

BABY FACE

Well, now you know all about the girls - but can you tell which is which from the baby pictures below? The info may give you little clues. Answers are on page 119.

a) I can't remember this photo being taken. In fact, I can't remember much until I was three. That was when my big adventure started!!

b) I was too young to remember this being taken - but it was at Christmas before my brother and sisters were around. Ah, I look lonely!

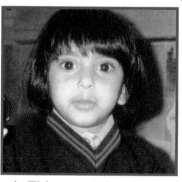

c) This was taken by my mum in our kitchen - but I don't remember what I was doing.

d) My mum took this picture and she thought it might have been on the day of my sister's birthday.

e) We were in town, so Mum took me into a shop where a photographer was doing a special promotion.

f) I don't remember this, but it was in our old house. My bedroom was very bright and I had lots of toys which I said hello to every morning.

56

Lonely!

Welcome to Dullsville, England

CARRIE CARTER, a thirteen-year-old from America, was making her first visit to Britain with her parents. While Mr Carter was at a conference in London, Carrie and her mother visited the village where Mrs Carter grew up.

Mum said I'd find it quiet and she wasn't wrong! There's nothing to do here. All the local kids must be away on vacation — and I don't blame them!

Then Carrie saw another reflection in the shop mirror.

Oh! Where did she come from? And what does she think she's staring at?

Hi! Having fun watching me?

Oh! I'm sorry! I — I thought you were someone I knew.

I don't think so. I'm Carrie Carter from America. I'm here on holiday with my mum.

I'm Kathryn and I live here. My best friend left England to go and live in America. I really miss her.

Perhaps we can be friends while I'm here this summer, Kathryn. I'm feeling pretty lonely, too.

Yes, I'd like that!

Just then Carrie's mum arrived —

Hiya, Carrie! Sorry to be so long but it took me ages to buy the groceries.

Hi, Mum!

Great! She's just in time to meet Kathryn!

But —

Oh! That's strange! Kathryn's gone. She *was* a bit shy, though!

Come on, Carrie! Get a move on!

Carrie and her mum were renting a house on the edge of the village.

It's a bit quiet in the village, Mum, but I met a girl there who's about the same age as me.

That's great, Carrie. I was afraid you might get bored. It's all changed since I lived here. My old house has gone and so have most of the people I knew.

However, today I found out that one of my old neighbours is in a home a few miles down the coast.

Are you thinking of going to visit her?

58

I've already arranged it. You can come too — or stay here with your new friend. I'm sure Mrs Weir could arrange a picnic lunch for you.

Cool!

I'd be delighted to, Mrs Carter.

So, next morning —

Have a nice day, dear. Don't go up on the clifftop path, though. It's not safe.

Don't worry, Mrs Weir. I won't go any further than the beach.

Kathryn was already on the beach waiting for Carrie —

I'm really looking forward to our picnic on the beach. We can go paddling and look for shells.

How does Kathryn know about the picnic? I meant it to be a surprise!

We've lots of great beaches in California where I come from. Where about in America did your friend move to, Kathryn?

She went to New York, Cara.

Far away across the sea . . . I never saw her again . . .

It's weird the way Kathryn's gazing out to sea — and that's not the first time she's called me Cara!

Next day on the beach, Carrie saw Kathryn crying —

What's wrong, Kathryn? Does that name you've written, Cara, make you unhappy?

Cara was the name of my best friend — the one who went away . . .

It's very like *my* name. I'm Caroline but because that's my mum's name, too, I get called Carrie.

How strange! I've got the same name as my mother, too. I'm glad you came here. I'll be so lonely when you leave.

The days flew by, then —

Your dad's conference has finished early, so we've to meet him in London tomorrow. He says he's got a surprise for us. We'd better start packing.

I'll go down to the beach and tell Kathryn I'm leaving then, Mum.

I'll come and get you in a few minutes, love. I'd like to meet this friend of yours.

Okay, Mum. I'll see you soon.

Carrie rushed off to see Kathryn —

Before you leave, Carrie, why don't we have a last walk together?

How on earth does she know I'm leaving? What's going on?

Let's explore the clifftops. There's a path that runs along the top.

I've been warned off the clifftops, Kathryn. They're not safe.

Please, Cara, there's still time. Come with me to the top of the cliffs!

I'm not going anywhere near the clifftop, Kathryn, and I'm Carrie, not Cara!

Carrie!

There's my mum! She wants to meet you before we go.

That's strange, Mum! Kathryn's gone! She was acting kinda weird before you showed!

Perhaps she just didn't want to say goodbye, Carrie. Come on, let's go back up to the house and pack.

Later that evening —

Mum, are you okay? You've been out here for ages.

I was just thinking about the past, Carrie. I was thinking about a good friend I had when I was a girl.

Shortly after I'd gone to America, I heard that my best friend had died. She'd been on the cliff path, gazing out to sea, when the path crumbled and she fell to her death. That's why the cliff path is kept closed.

Aw, Mum, that's such a sad story.

We were inseparable when we were young — Katy and Cara, the terrible twosome.

Katy and Cara?

I was known as Cara when I was younger. My friend Katy was the same. Her proper name was Kathryn.

The Kathryn I met had a friend called Cara who went to America! And she wanted me to walk on the clifftop where Mum's friend died! Did she want me to die, too, so I could never leave her?

No, it must just be a coincidence. Kathryn said her friend went to New York. It's all this talk of the past that's spooked me and made me think I've met the ghost of Mum's old friend.

Next day, Carrie and her mum met up with her dad —

It's been a good holiday but I can't wait to get back to our Californian sunshine.

You'll have to wait a few more days yet, honey. I've arranged an extra stop at New York for us all.

New York? Why?

That's where Kathryn said her friend went!

My family lived in New York first of all when we moved to America. Then we eventually settled in California.

So your mum will have the chance to visit even more of her old haunts!

So Cara *did* leave Kathryn behind and go to New York! Maybe it *was* the ghost of Mum's old friend that I made friends with — I'll never know!

the end

Are you a perfect star?

You're funny and adventurous, but easily annoyed. Are you a perfect Aries, Cancer, Aquarius or Virgo? Find out with our fun quiz!

START
Do you always get your own way?

Is coming up with new ideas easy for you?

Can you tell jokes?

Is trying new things frightening?

Are you good at making decisions?

Can you be grumpy sometimes?

Do people sometimes tell you to cheer up?

Do silly things make you laugh?

Are you an animal lover?

You love swimming. True?

Are you always helping friends?

Is solving problems easy for you?

Do you prefer books to parties?

You spend ages choosing presents. True?

You're probably a FIRE sign - Aries, Leo or Sagittarius. You're famous for being full of fun, but also quick to let others know when you're not happy. You make an interesting and loyal friend.

You're showing all the signs of being an EARTH sign such as Taurus, Virgo or Capricorn. You're a great friend - always ready to help others, but you can also be very stubborn.

You're most like the WATER signs of Cancer, Scorpio or Pisces. You're creative, caring and sharing, but bad at making any decisions. This can drive your mates mad!

It's possible you're an AIR sign like Gemini, Libra or Aquarius. You're quiet and kind and don't like surprises, but make a fab, thoughtful friend. You may be very artistic or musical.

63

Continued from page 10

DONNA GREEN'S mum had just had a win on the lottery —

Penny's Place

Hmm. Ma looks different today. The lottery win seems to have put her in a good mood.

'Bye, Donna. See you!

No, it's more than that. She really suits her hair in that new style — and she's wearing a load of new clothes. Oh, I hope she's not spending *all* the winnings.

So, later —

Spend all the money? No way, Donna. I've just bought a couple of new tops. Gotta look smart for work, after all.

Yeah, I guess.

Now, pet, what is it? Your usual?

Yep! Full breakfast and a mug of your special tea, darling.

Darling? Yeuch! What a creep!

A couple of days later —

That's not another new top is it, Ma?

What, this old thing? I've had it for ages, Sharon.

Huh?

Am I imagining things, Donna, or has your ma smartened herself up a bit lately?

Well spotted, Pa. Ma says she has to look good now she's manager at the café.

You reckon? Hmm! You don't think she's got herself a boyfriend, do you?

Nah! But I wouldn't really blame her if she did. It wouldn't do any harm for *you* to smarten yourself up a bit.

I think you're right, our Donna. I-I've been plannin' to get a new image for a while, now.

Wow! That'd be a cool Chrissie pressie! *Two* smart parents!

So —

Are you wearing aftershave, Pa Green?

I certainly am, my love. Does anyone have a problem with it?

No. It's a definite improvement.

But, a few days later —

You don't think your pa's up to something, do you, Donna?

No. He's just smartened himself up a bit, Ma.

Donna told her mates —

How long do you think your pa will keep it up?

Don't know. At least till Christmas, I hope!

Then —

There you are, love. Your usual. Now I'll grab a quick break.

Sit down and join me, darling. I could do with a bit of company.

What's she playing at? She's flirting with him.

Dave's like that with everyone, Donna. He's just being friendly.

Huh! He looks more than friendly. Mum hasn't *really* got a boyfriend, has she? Some Christmas pressie *that* would be!

Just then —

Oh, *very* cosy. Now I see why you've bought all those clothes. Got a new *friend*, have you?

Eh?

Calm down, mate. We're only having a laugh.

You're a fine one to talk! This sudden change of image doesn't fool me. You're up to something, Dan Green.

Oh, no. Everyone's staring.

You're nothing but a rotten cheat, I . . .

Get them into the back shop. It'll be more private there.

So —

I'll hold the fort, Mrs Green.

Crazy man! I'm out of here!

This row could go on for ages. Now all the family will have a miserable Christmas.

Don't worry, Donna, your folks always sort things out. I bet your Christmas will be heaps better than mine!

Now all that was left was working out what to buy for Christmas presents —

I'm skint — as usual. But Ma's using the last of her winnings to treat us to a meal out on Christmas Day.

I've got your pressies already, cos I'm off to London tomorrow.

I wonder what *I'll* be doing? Serving next door, I expect. Mum will probably have to do a special Christmas Day deal for her up-market customers. Everything revolves around the business these days.

And, soon —

Sorry about that little mix up, girls. Time I went back to work, Cuddles.

Of course. I'll see you at home, Pumpkin.

Phew! Peace at last!

Thanks, Sita. What about you, Arlene?

Actually, we're *all* spending the day at Dad's. Even Mum. It'll be nice to have a family Christmas again!

But —

Hmm. Takings are down. I think my customers at 'Penny's' are too busy Christmas shopping to have time for coffee and snacks.

'Penny's Place' is still thriving, though.

68

Games For A Laugh!

Tired of TV? Bored with board games? Well, we've got some suggestions for things to do and games to play that'll mean hours of fun for you and your mates. So get phoning them **now**!

FAME GAME

Write the names of six famous people or characters from TV on separate strips of paper. Fold the strips so no one can read the names, put them into a bowl and mix them up. Divide yourselves into two teams - you can wear silly team badges if you like! Then, alternating between the two teams, each player takes out a strip and describes the person or character without naming them. The other team tries to guess who it is. When all the strips have been used, they are re-folded and put back in the bowl. In round two, you do the same as the first round but this time you are allowed only three words to describe who's on the paper. In the last round, you have to act out the name without saying anything.

LET'S MAKE UP!

If everyone brings a bag of their own make-up, then you can practise using the wildest colours and styles you can think of. You're only limited by your imagination! Be outrageous - spray your hair different colours (using wash-out sprays, of course), add hair clips or scrunchies to the maddest hairstyles you can think of. Paint your toenails and fingernails all different colours. Then you can paint designs on your face with lipstick or eyeshadow - it'll wash off later! A finishing touch could be to dress up in crazy clothes. Be wild!

SCARED STIFF!

Who doesn't like telling spooky stories? And if you're having a sleepover, it's the ideal time to tell ghost stories. When you're all tucked up in bed, take turns to tell a story. Sound effects are always good, too! But don't get too carried away or you might not be able to sleep afterwards!

WHO AM I?

All you need for this game is sticky paper and pens. Give everyone a piece of sticky paper and ask them to write down the name of a famous person. You can limit this to pop stars or film stars or even just people you know personally. Whatever you do, don't let the friend on your right see what you write because you'll be sticking the paper with the name on it to her forehead! The idea is that you ask questions which can only be answered by a "yes" or "no", to try to discover who you are! You can keep asking questions for as long as the answers are yes. As soon as you get a "no", the next person takes a turn. Keep going until you all guess your names - or get fed up trying!

DON'T SHOUT!

You have to have a good memory for this game! Imagine you're going on holiday and you're packing your case. The first person says, "I packed my suitcase and in it I put..." and she adds something she would pack. The next person repeats the same sentence, including what's packed, and then adds another item. This goes on, adding items all the way. If you forget any of the items, or say them out of order, you're out and it goes to the next player. Usually, the volume of this game gets louder and louder!

CLEVER CAT!

Another game which can get quite noisy is The Minister's Cat. The first player says, "The minister's cat is an adventurous cat" or uses another adjective which begins with an "A". Then, quickly but in turn, all the other players have to describe the cat with a different adjective starting with the same letter. When everyone has had a turn, the person who was second begins with a new letter - all the way through the alphabet. If at any time you can't think of a word right away, you drop out. Start swotting up on your adjectives now!

71

Let's visit... SPAIN

Countless Costas!

Beaches

Sea, sun and sand! It's what Spain is famous for. From built-up beaches where the fun never stops, to quiet coves where you can hide from holiday hordes - they're all to be found in Spain. And thanks to the Balearic and Canary Islands there's even more sizzlin' Spanish seaside scenery for us to enjoy!

Food

Mmm!

If we were to judge Spanish food on what we eat on holiday, we'd probably think all Spaniards ate chips, burgers, pizzas(!) and 'full English breakfasts'. Think again. Real Spanish food is delicious and uses lots of fresh fruit and vegetables – as well as fish and meat. Try Spanish Omelette (tortilla) or paella – or how about tapas? These are small portions served in individual dishes and you can choose exactly what you want. Mmmm!

Quick Quiz

(Answers on page 119)

How often do the words SEA, SUN and SAND appear in our mini search?

```
s e a s
a u e n
n a n u
d n a s
```

Which is larger, Minorca or Majorca?

What does 'adios' mean?

Disney

Disney or not?

Although there are some great water and fun parks to visit in Spain, there isn't a Disney park as such - at least, not yet! However, one place *does* have Disney connections - and that is the turreted alcazar (castle) in Segovia. Some people say that Walt Disney modelled Cinderella's castle on this very building. Visit it and see what *you* think.

Fiestas

Spaniards love parties, so they will find a reason to hold a fiesta at the drop of a hat. (Sombrero, perhaps?) There are lots of special days and carnivals throughout the year, when the whole town or village joins in the celebrations. Dancing, music, eating - it's fiesta-fabby!

Shopping

Tourist shops in Spain are packed with all the goodies you could ever want – and a lot you will *never* want, too. Top things to buy include jewellery and ceramic ornaments. Little Spanish figures are cute – and cheap, too – so why not start a collection?

Cheap and cheerful.

Spanish Sizzlers
They put the sparkle in Spain.

Oranges

Tomatoes

Tortilla

Enrique Iglesias

Guitars

Castanets

Football

Flamenco Dancing

Olives

Did you know...?

* The famous Spanish Steps are not in Spain - they're in Rome.
* Spain is bordered by Portugal, France and tiny Andorra.
* The capital city, Madrid, is the highest capital in Europe.

Use Your Loaf
Bread recipes from around the world

TAPAS
Lots of tapas use bread as a base and, while they may sound simple, they are delicious - and easy to make. Try these.

WARM BREAD WITH GARLIC
Use a good quality loaf and warm it in the oven. Cut into thickish slices and rub each with a peeled clove of garlic. Drizzle a little olive oil on each, and eat!
Variations
Prepare the bread as above but, instead of drizzling with oil, top with slices of roasted peppers, olive paste, tomatoes, cheese or - best of all - good quality Spanish ham.

SARDINE SLICE
Cut the bread into pieces big enough to hold a sardine. Grill the bread on both sides then top with a slice of onion and a sardine (in tomato sauce or oil). Season and serve with a slice of lemon.

Always ask an adult's permission before using kitchen equipment.

Kangaroos

*Red Kangaroos can't see very clearly when close up, but can spot movements at great distances. Wonder how they recognise each other?

*Western Grey and Eastern Grey Kangaroos are different species. The Western Greys are native to the west (and parts of the south) of Australia, while the Eastern Greys come from the – er – east! Now there's a surprise.

*Thanks to their colour, Red Kangaroos can merge into their background. This means they can be very hard to spot in the dry Australian outback.

*Eastern Kangaroos have coarser and curlier hair than those from the west. Mmmm! Not much we can say about that, really.

*Kangaroos tend to stay in dry areas, rather than go near wet grasslands. With their big flat feet, they might easily get stuck in bogs.

*Kangaroos like to rest during the day and eat late at night. How posh!

Have you ever wondered what it was like going to school in Victorian times? Becky Taverner did, so we took her along to *Hitchin's British Schools Trust* where she soon found out.

CLASS ACT!

1. Hitchin's is a 'living museum' set in a real Victorian school building. When the school opened in 1837 it was only boys who were pupils, but now girls can play their part, too. First Becky met Lois, whose grandma was going to be teacher for the day. Then she was given a pinafore to wear over her clothes, so she really looked the part.

2. In the classroom the desks are tiered so teacher can see *everyone* all the time. Gulp!

3. Time for lessons. But what's a farthing?

4. Hands have to be inspected to make sure they won't leave dirty marks on the school books. Stop smiling, girls. This is serious!

5. Punishment was harsh. Becky's been caught slouching over her desk so has to wear a back straightener, while another pupil, Adam, has to wear the dunce's cap and sit facing a wall. His crime? He couldn't name all Queen Victoria's children.

6. Next it's writing with pen, and ink from an inkwell. Becky soons realises why you need blotting paper and a cloth to wipe away the excess ink. Teacher warns everyone not to cross their nibs or blot their copybooks - that would mean *big* trouble!

7. At playtime the girls head outside for a game of hopscotch. Come on, girls. Stop posing and get hoppin'!

8. Now *more* lessons. This time it's nature study. Today the class is going to look at the life of a squirrel.

9. The little ones have fun making shapes in a sand tray - while Becky and the others use slates.

10. There's even time for keep fit. In Victorian times it was known as 'physical jerks'. Arms out . . . one, two, three, four . . .

11. Becky inspects a *huge* bar of soap! Adam explains that families would cut a slice from the huge carbolic bar each week. It doesn't half pong!

12. Each child had to pay a penny a week for lessons - and Becky's no exception.

So, do you still think Victorian school would be fun? If so, you can find out more by visiting Hitchin's British Schools Trust yourself. Phone 01462 452697 for further details. And what did Becky think? She loved her visit to Victorian times - but is happy to stick to her *own* school from now on.

Always ask permission from the person who pays the bill before phoning.

Work it out!

Get out of that!

Follow the right path to get to your friend's house. She's waiting, so don't take too long!

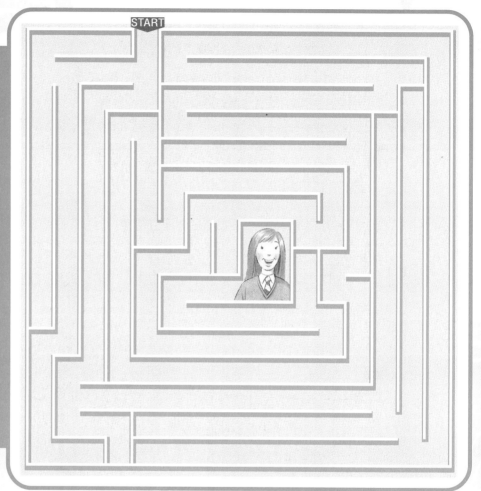

START

Love or Hate?

Fill in the grid by using the clues. The answers are all things you probably love or *hate*! When you fill in all the answers, the letters in the coloured panel spell out something that *everyone* loves!

1. You have to go there for lessons.
2. Something sweet and yummy to eat.
3. Slimy black creatures - yuck!
4. We all love to dress up and go to these.
5. They're eight-legged and hairy - yikes!
6. It makes you wet and miserable!
7. Another name for lads.
8. You like to dance to this.

78

What Are They?

These are all things you will recognise, but they've been photographed from odd angles. Can you see what they are?

1

2

3

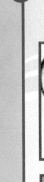

4

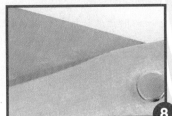

5

6

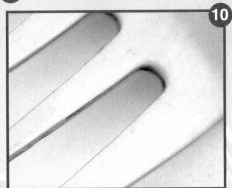

7

8

9

10

11

12

What Order?

Below is a list of things you probably do in the morning. Put them in the correct order.

Have shower

Switch off alarm clock

Go to school

Get dressed

Wake up

Get out of bed

Making Words

Chat about the latest things you've been up to. How many words of three letters or more can you make from the word **CHATTERBOX**?

1-12 You're not really trying, are you?

13-25 Not bad, not bad!

26+ Impressive!

Answers on page 119

Pictures posed by models.

LOST FOR WO

✳ You're showing off your new T-shirt when someone points to a stain on the front. Instead of blushing, why not try one of these responses?

Miss Superior
"Stain?" you smile sweetly. "That's part of the pattern. I thought *everyone* knew that!"

Miss Couldn't Care Less
Giggle and say, *"So that's where my breakfast landed."*

Miss Smart
"Yes," you say, quick as a flash. "It's just like the one *you* had on your shirt last week."

✳ You get top marks in the maths test at school and someone calls you a swot. Try hitting back with one of these comments.

Miss Couldn't Care Less
"So what? There's nothing wrong with swotting - not if you want to do well."

Miss Smart
"Unlike some people, *I* don't have to count on my fingers."

Miss Superior
"Swot? I never have to swot *anything* - it all comes naturally."

✳ You find that you've got to wear specs to school and, on your first day, someone calls you four-eyes. Here are some replies to make you feel better.

Miss Smart

"Actually," you say, "I've only got *two* eyes. If you can't see that then *you* obviously need your eyes tested."

Miss Superior

"You noticed?" you reply. "Just like Madonna and Britney. They've got glasses exactly like mine!"

Miss Couldn't Care Less

"Yeah. And now I don't bump into lampposts or ignore my friends in the street."

✳ You stick a picture of your fave star on your book, but someone picks it up and says "Yeugh! He's horrible!". Don't get angry, get even with one of these remarks.

Miss Couldn't Care Less

"Everyone has different tastes. And I think he's *gorgeous*!"

Miss Smart

"Looks aren't the most important thing - luckily for *you*!"

Miss Superior

"Oh, I don't just go on looks. I've met him and he's *such* a nice person."

RDs?

If someone makes a cutting comment, can you *never* think of a good reply - until it's much too late, that is? If so, then maybe we can help!

✳ Your mother comes to collect you from school, and someone calls you "mummy's girl". Here's what you could say in reply.

Miss Superior

"'Bye. I'll wave to you as we pass the bus!"

Miss Smart

"Do you know, before you said that, we were going to offer you a lift."

Miss Couldn't Care Less

"It beats walking or getting the bus."

✳ You're the tallest girl in the class, and a boy calls you a giraffe. Don't worry. Cut him down to size by saying one of these.

Miss Smart

"And what are *you* then, shorty! A shrimp?"

Miss Couldn't Care Less

"Yeah - just like the super models."

Miss Superior

"Being tall is great. It means I can look down on lowlife like you!"

in colour!

Miss-Chievous

Danielle's cool colouring - bright blue eyes and blonde hair - means she suits the colours of blue skies, the yellow sun and the rainbow colours of summer flowers.

*Colours for *you* to wear, if you share Danielle's colouring, are blue, green and pastel pinks and purples.
*Denim and bright *'jewel'* colours can look cool, too.
*Black also gives a great *contrast* with blonde hair.

In our first outfit, we dressed Danielle from head to toe in *blue* - her favourite colour! "I *loved* the blue jumper top!" she told us. We gave Danielle's eyes a dramatic look for this outfit, using purple eyeshadow with a little bit of blue at the corners.

To match Danielle's second outfit - a pale pink top and brown trousers, we used pink tones on her cheeks and pinky-purple on her eyes. "I don't wear much make up - usually just blues and silvers," Danielle told us. "But I'll try these colours at home. I like them because I think they make me look older."

*Blondes tend to suit gold jewellery and accessories - it goes well with their golden skin tone.
*Blondes can get away with almost any colour - so go for rainbows!
*If you can't find hair bobbles to match what you're wearing, you can use bead bracelets instead. That's what we did for Danielle's pink outfit.

The Lucky Locket

CHARLOTTE had spent her life in an orphanage but now it was time for her to leave.

A Mandy Classic from 1992

Matron says I'm to be scullery-maid at Graveley Hall, Harriet. I'll miss you, after all these years.

You've been a good lass, Charlotte. I always said you were special.

You said, 'You never know with an orphan' — as if I might be a princess.

Ha, ha — well you never *do* know! Now, I'd like you to have this.

A locket! I've never seen anything so beautiful! Where did you get it, Harriet?

It was tucked in your shawl the night we found you — that and a bit of paper with your name — Charlotte.

"I kept it safe for you, my love. Don't sell it until you're desperate."

"Oh, I won't *ever* sell it, Harriet — it's far too precious."

"This must be my mother — we have the same dark hair and eyes. Why did she leave me — and where is she now?"

Next day —

"What a big place! Perhaps I'll be happy here, after all. Maybe my locket will bring me luck."

"Here is your new scullery-maid, Cook."

"Thanks, Miss Murdoch — I hope she lasts longer than the last brat!"

Charlotte was soon hard at work —

"After that, Maggie will show you the pails and brushes. I want the scullery floor sparkling clean."

"Charlotte's too posh a name for a scullery-maid. I'll call you 'Lowly' — cos that's what you are, the lowest of the low!"

Charlotte struggled free.

I've got to get away! They *mustn't* get the locket!

You just wait, Lowly!

Soon —

I seem to have lost them, thank goodness. Oh, what a mess I look.

Please, sir — what will you give me for this? I know it's worth a lot of money.

Hmmmm . . .

Just then —

Grab her! Whatever she's got, she must have stolen it.

I *didn't* steal it — it was my mother's!

This *lady* — the mother of a dirty urchin like *you?* Save your lies for the law, my girl!

No, sir, I beg you — I speak the truth!

Poor Charlotte was taken before a magistrate —

I didn't steal it, sir! You can ask Harriet, at Borton Orphanage, if you don't believe me. She knows all about it.

Hmm! Very well — this case is adjourned, so that this Harriet person can be traced. Take her away.

That night —

What a horrible place. But I shan't have to stay long, once they've spoken to Harriet.

But, two days later —

The old woman, Harriet, died a few weeks ago. With no evidence to the contrary, the prisoner is found guilty of theft, and shall be jailed.

No! Please no!

After several weeks locked in her cell, Charlotte had given up all hope. Then, one day, a warder took her to a small room, where a lady was waiting.

She was a stranger and she gazed at Charlotte with eyes full of sadness — and hope. Then she spoke in a foreign accent.

Please, do not be nervous, my child. If I could ask, would you be so kind as to show me your left shoulder?

W-why?

Do as the lady asks, girl!

There it is! The family birthmark. Oh, my dear — I think I must tell you a little story. Come, sit down.

91

The story began in France, twelve years earlier, with a young lady giving her parents some unwelcome news.

You wish to marry my head groom? Are you mad, daughter?

How could you be happy, married to a servant?

I *love* Pierre. Riches mean nothing.

That night —

Oh, Pierre — running away will break my parents' hearts.

It is the only way we can be together, my love. We will be safe in England. We will return in a few years.

In England, Pierre found work in the stables of a big house. He and Adele were poor but happy — especially after their daughter was born.

I could not be more content, my love.

I, too, husband. And soon we will return to France. I'm sure my parents will forgive us now!

But one day —

. . . the horse reared and its hoof struck your husband on the side of the head. He died instantly, I'm afraid.

No!

I'm sorry, lass. You will be given compensation, but I'm afraid you must leave the cottage by the end of the week.

But, where will I go with my baby? Oh, Pierre — my Pierre!

Poor Adele searched for work, but no-one would employ a widow with a baby. Soon, her money ran out and she had no choice but to leave her child on the steps of an orphanage.

There, my baby. I will return when I have earned enough money to take us to France.

93

"A NAIL party? What's that?" Mandy asked her cousin, Zoe. The girls lived just around the corner from each other, and were in the same class at school.

"It's the latest thing from America. Everyone brings different coloured nail varnishes and you all do each others' nails."

"It sounds great," said Mandy.

"Why don't we do it as a joint birthday party?" Zoe suggested. "You invite six friends, and I'll invite six."

"Okay," smiled Mandy, "as long as you don't invite Sharon Spiker!"

"Oh, she's not my friend any more," Zoe replied. "She said something mean about Kitchia and her kittens, so I'm definitely not inviting her!"

the nail party

And, when Zoe and Mandy held their party at Zoe's three weeks later, Sharon was nowhere to be seen.

"Who wants to go first?" asked Zoe. "Mum and Dad gave me a fab basket of fourteen different nail varnishes, so we've got loads of choice — look!"

...everyone gasped.

"What a lovely basket," said Jenny, but then everyone gasped. For in the basket were not fourteen pretty little circular bottles, but four. Zoe was almost in tears.

"I only opened it last night," she croaked. "Where can the other bottles be?"

"They must be somewhere," said Mandy. "Look, why don't we start with the coloured bangles and beads your mum gave me and we can search for the nail varnishes later?" And Mandy explained about the kit with beads, letters and numbers that could be used to make up necklaces, before holding p her box of goodies for veryone to see.

Once again, a gasp of orror went around the oom. The letters looked s if they were all there, nd the numbers, but all he beads were missing.

"This is just too much," aid Zoe. "Someone's rying to spoil our party. ut how did they do it? My ail varnishes and your ead kit were here, in the ouse, all night."

"Yeah, but they were itting in the porch," said Mandy. "The milkman or ostman could have ot them."

"What would the milkman or postman want with nail varnish and eads?" said Zoe sharply. No, this was done by omeone with a grudge."

"Like someone who vasn't invited," suggested Jenny.

"We'll never find out who it was!"

"But loads of people weren't invited," said Mandy. "We'll never find ut who it was!"

Just then, Zoe's mum came bustling into the oom, carrying Zoe's baby sister, Sophie. She held out yet another birthday card.

"I forgot to tell you, Zoe," she smiled. "While you were shopping this morning, a friend of yours

dropped round with this card."

Zoe looked at it suspiciously, then threw it down in disgust.

"I might have guessed. It's from Sharon Spiker. Did she stay long, Mum?"

"No. She just came into the porch to give me this, then she went away. Anyway, Zoe, I mustn't disturb you," and Zoe's mum bustled out of the room with Sophie.

"So!" snorted Abigail, "Sharon came here with the excuse of giving you a card, and took the opportunity to mess up our party!"

"Wait a moment," said Mandy, stooping to pick something from the floor. "I think Sophie dropped this." She waved something in the air.

"You've got it all wrong!"

"Look what I've found," she cried. It was a large letter 'a' in bright red wood.

"It's one of the missing necklace pieces. Sophie must have messed them up."

Zoe went bright red with annoyance. How dare Mandy criticise her baby sister! Then she examined the letter more closely.

"You've got it all wrong," she said. "The letters in your box are all there — and they're smaller, too. This is one of Sophie's alphabet toys." This time it was Mandy's turn to go bright red — with embarrassment.

Before anyone could say anything else, there was a loud rattling at the door. Surely it couldn't be Sharon Spiker!

Zoe rushed over and opened the door. And, there, chasing each other round the room excitedly were Zoe's cat, Kitchia, and her kittens, all playing football with the missing beads and nail varnish!

The girls burst out laughing.

"They must have clawed the bottles and beads out of the basket," said Abigail. "Looks like the mystery of the missing nail varnish is solved at last."

The End

Who's your perfect pal?

Should you be best friends with a Scorpio, Taurus, Libra or Leo? The answers are in the stars - and this quick quiz!

START

Do you have lots of patience? Y / N

Are you happiest indoors? Y / N

Making decisions is difficult for you. True? Y / N

Is shopping a fave hobby? N / Y

Is art your top school subject? Y / N

Are you good at keeping secrets? Y / N

Do you love chocolate? N / Y

Do you cry easily? Y

Would friends come to you for advice? Y / N

Do you have more than one best friend? N / Y

Are you good at sharing? N / Y

Are you always on time? Y / N

Are you a TV addict? Y / N

Are you very organised? N / Y

You've followed the path to Cancer, Scorpio and Pisces. These WATER signs will make perfect pals who will always pick you the perfect presents and give endless advice on what to wear.

You should get on very well with AIR signs like Gemini, Libra and Aquarius. Interested in the arty side of life, you'll admire their weird outfits, but not want to wear them yourself!

FIRE signs like Aries, Leo and Sagittarius are the perfect pals for you. You'll share their sense of adventure but could find their constant chatting annoying at times.

The down to EARTH signs of Taurus, Virgo and Capricorn will be great mates. They'll always try to help you out of sticky situations but you won't get them to change their minds.

PAULA'S sister could be really annoying —

That's my new top you're wearing, Sally. Where did you get it?

From your wardrobe, of course! I didn't think you'd mind.

The Borrower

Well I *do*! I was going to wear it tonight.

What's the big deal?

She's loads of other stuff to wear, Mum!

That's enough, Sally. Go upstairs and take that top off *now!*

Don't worry, Paula. I'll wash and dry your top. It'll be ready for you going out.

Thanks, Mum. I hate Sally borrowing my things without asking.

98

That's us off, then. Tell Gran if you go out, and take your front door keys so you don't disturb her when you come back.

Okay, Mum. Have a nice meal.

'Bye!

That's me done. Fancy going to the youth club, Paula?

Not tonight, Sally. This French is going to take me ages.

Okay. I'll go and get ready. And don't worry, I'll remember to speak to Gran and take my key!

Right. I'll see you later, Sally.

But, after half an hour —

I won't be long, Gran, but you can call me on my mobile if you need me.

Okay, love. Remember to lock the door when you go out.

That was easier than I expected. I think I might pop round to Marie's for a while.

101

I was a bit grumpy with Sally this morning, but she's really annoying, Paula!

Tell me about it! I'll swap you her for your brother!

No chance! I . . .

Oh, my phone's ringing.

Okay, Gran. Don't worry. I'll be with you soon.

My gran's feeling dizzy, Marie, so I'd better go. I'll see you tomorrow.

Okay, Paula, I hope your gran's okay.

So do I. Last time Gran felt dizzy, she ended up in hospital.

Then —

Oh, no! Where's my key? It's *always* in my purse!

Gran! Gran! It's me — Paula! Let me in!

Oh, no! She's collapsed. It looks like she's unconscious.

Paula dashed next door —

It's my gran, Mrs Davis. She's collapsed and I can't find my key!

Don't worry, Paula. You phone the doctor and I'll see if there's a window open or something.

Soon —

How is she, Doctor?

Not too bad — but I'd like her to go into hospital for a few checks. An ambulance is on its way.

When the ambulance had gone —

Thank goodness you phoned us, Paula.

And thank goodness Mrs Davis managed to break in. I wish I knew what happened to my key.

Hi, everyone! You're home early. Hey, I saw an ambulance a few minutes ago. Did I miss something exciting?

It was hardly exciting. Gran's been taken to hospital.

Paula explained —

. . . I'd lost my key and I couldn't get in!

Oh, no! I — I took it!

I couldn't find my own key, so I took Paula's. I didn't think anyone would notice.

Oh, Sally! If you'd told me, I could have borrowed Gran's.

I hope this teaches you a lesson! You're grounded for the next month!

Mum went to the hospital —

I — I'm really sorry, Paula.

Poor Sally. If I weren't so worried about Gran, I'd feel sorry for *her*.

Then —

That's great news, Mum. See you later.

What's great news? Is Gran okay?

Yeah! She's going to be fine, Sally.

Thank goodness. I really *am* sorry, Paula. I promise I'll *never* borrow anything again — well, not without asking.

I'll hold you to that. Now, any chance I can 'borrow' my key back? After all, you're not going to be needing it, are you?

That's true! But you know what, Paula? It serves me right!

THE END

in colour!

Hannah has warm colouring - golden skin tone, brown eyes and brown hair - and so suits the colours of spring and autumn.

*Top colours to choose if *you* have warm colouring are bright reds, blues, greens and oranges.
*Colours to *avoid* are some shades of purple, yellow and brown.
*Surprisingly, *white* is also a colour which suits brunettes. The contrast between light and dark can be very striking.

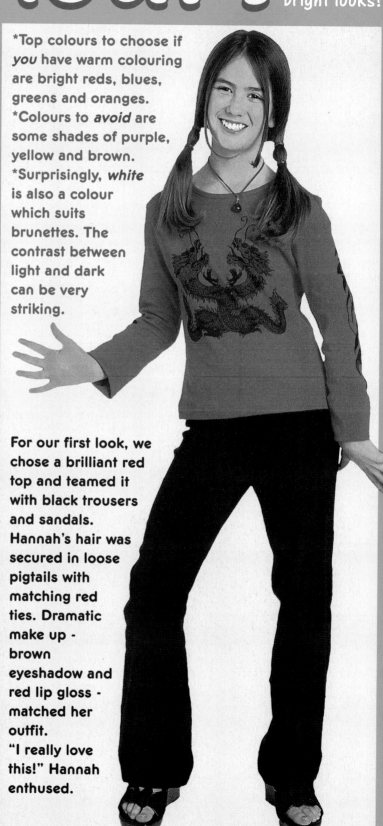

For our first look, we chose a brilliant red top and teamed it with black trousers and sandals. Hannah's hair was secured in loose pigtails with matching red ties. Dramatic make up - brown eyeshadow and red lip gloss - matched her outfit.
"I really love this!" Hannah enthused.

106

*Girls with Hannah's colouring are very lucky. They suit both natural and dramatic make up.
We gave Hannah a natural look - pale pink eyeshadow and pearly lip gloss - to go with her next outfit - a cool blue top and dusky pink cords. Blue and pink hair ties finished her look.
Hannah loved it all.
"I normally wear sparkly gold make up, so trying something different was great."

*Silver jewellery and accessories look striking on brunettes. Here, a silver clasp shows up well against Hannah's dark hair.
*Brightly coloured accessories will look good, too.
*Brown hair reflects light and is usually very shiny.

Your Year!

What lies ahead for you this year?
It's all in your stars – so read on!

ARIES
MAR 22 - APR 20
You'll find it difficult to keep a secret, but you must! When a friend asks you for advice, you'll surprise everyone with a fab idea for helping them!

TAURUS
APR 21 - MAY 21
Interesting family news could cause quite a few changes in February or March. The rest of the year will be taken up with a cool new hobby.

GEMINI
MAY 22 - JUNE 21
A friend or family member may be on the move, but don't worry, they won't end up too far away. You may be jealous of a pal's cute new pet.

CANCER
JUNE 22 - JULY 23
Some kind of prize could be coming your way at school - wow! A new friend you make in the summer could upset a mate, so take care.

LEO
JULY 24 - AUG 23
You'll discover a hidden talent and impress quite a few people in the second half of the year. A change in appearance looks likely in May.

VIRGO
AUG 24 - SEPT 23
There's a big decision to be made, so you'll have to give it lots of thought. Once you've made up your mind, the rest of the year will be fun!

LIBRA
SEPT 24 - OCT 23
A new arrival at school could cause quite a stir, but things should quickly settle down. You may also find something you lost a long time ago!

SCORPIO
OCT 24 - NOV 22
The chance to go on an unexpected trip might lead to a flurry of activity around your birthday. Extra money could come your way in June.

SAGITTARIUS
NOV 23 - DEC 22
You may be jealous of a friend's good news, but something exciting's about to happen to you, too! You could be asked to a really cool concert!

CAPRICORN
DEC 23 - JAN 21
A friend's worry should turn out to be nothing too serious. You may be asked to help plan a surprise party in the summer for someone you like

AQUARIUS
JAN 22 - FEB 19
Don't take too long to make a decision or someone else could beat you to it! A big clear out may make you want to change the look of your room.

PISCES
FEB 20 - MAR 21
Planning a sleepover will keep you and your friends occupied for ages. It'll end up being brilliant! Be careful or you could lose something in July.

Puzzled?

Hidden in this giant wordsearch are things that you might find in your bedroom. Use the list below, ticking off each word as you find it in the grid. The words can read forwards, backwards, up, down or diagonally, and each letter can be used more than once.

T	H	G	I	L	J	C	S	H	O	E	S	C	S
D	P	U	E	K	A	M	U	L	O	E	I	U	R
N	R	O	D	B	J	J	A	R	R	V	T	S	E
N	O	E	S	C	O	M	P	U	T	E	R	H	P
I	B	R	S	T	P	R	T	M	V	A	M	I	P
G	M	D	N	S	E	C	D	U	H	Q	I	O	I
H	O	R	H	A	I	R	D	R	Y	E	R	N	L
T	C	A	E	P	M	N	S	B	A	N	R	S	S
I	D	M	K	Y	O	E	G	A	R	W	O	R	E
E	T	E	P	R	A	C	N	G	R	U	R	I	H
Z	T	C	U	D	D	L	Y	T	O	Y	S	A	T
C	E	M	U	F	R	E	P	U	S	W	O	H	O
F	P	Y	J	A	M	A	S	D	D	C	N	C	L
W	O	L	L	I	P	Y	C	K	C	O	L	C	C

BED
BRUSH
CARPET
CD PLAYER
CDS
CHAIR
CLOCK
CLOTHES
COMB
COMPUTER

CUDDLY TOYS
CURTAINS
CUSHION
DESK
DRESSING GOWN
DUVET
HAIRDRYER
LAMPSHADE
LIGHT
MAKEUP

MIRROR
NIGHTIE
ORNAMENTS
PERFUME
PICTURES
PILLOW
POSTERS
PYJAMAS
SHOES
SLIPPERS

109

Let's visit...
THE BRITISH ISLES

Yes, there are lots of places to go right here at home! Honestly!

Towering sights in London.

Cities

London, Edinburgh, Cardiff, Belfast, Dublin, Newcastle, Swansea, Glasgow, Douglas, York - there are dozens of cool cities to visit. London, in particular, has loads to offer. Walk across Tower Bridge, sail on the Thames, get lost in the Hampton Court maze or have a picnic in Hyde Park - the list is endless. Then there's shopping, of course........

Paula Radcliffe. A true Brit!

Sport

Football, cricket, tennis, skiing, athletics and loads more, the British love sports. Trouble is, with a few exceptions, we're not very good at them. Still, we do our best and it's the taking part that matters, after all — isn't it? And we do win sometimes!

Islands

We've got lots! From the Shetlands in the north to the Channel Islands in the south, there are islands of all shapes and sizes. And where there are islands, there are also boats. So, if you like sailing, then this is a fabby place to live! We're not short of mountains, either, so if climbing's your thing, then you're in luck.

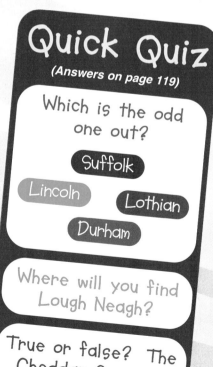

Quick Quiz
(Answers on page 119)

Which is the odd one out?

Suffolk

Lincoln   Lothian

Durham

Where will you find Lough Neagh?

True or false? The Cheddar Gorge is made from cheese.

Brill Brits

Here's what makes us 'Great'.

Blue – top popsters.

- Weather
- Tartan
- Pop music
- Shamrocks
- Daffodils
- Nessie
- The Queen
- Tea

Food

Tea and scones. How British!

We Brits are certainly versatile when it comes to food. Anything from pies to pizza, tandoori to tripe, hash browns to haggis - and don't forget good old bangers, burgers, and afternoon tea, of course. It may not be the healthiest cuisine around, but it's certainly varied.

Beaches

Small coves, surfing sites, long stretches of soft golden sands, pebble beaches and narrow, grey sea fronts – we've got the lot! Unfortunately, the weather isn't always perfect! However, on a warm sunny day in summer, some of our beaches are hard to beat. But pack your brolly – just in case!

Sunscreen, bug repellent, sunglasses – and brolly. A British picnic kit!

Did You Know?

* The highest mountain is Ben Nevis.
* Cornwall has its own flag. It's black with a white cross.
* Britain is best - so there!!!

Use Your Loaf

Bread recipes from around the world

WELSH RAREBIT
Rarebit or rabbit, you can call it what you like. One thing that can't be argued about is this - it's a cheese-lover's dream

Ingredients:
2–4 slices of bread
50g grated Cheddar cheese
2 tablespoons of milk
A little butter
½ teaspoon of mustard
Pepper to taste

Method:
Melt the cheese and milk in a saucepan with the mustard and pepper, being careful to stir all the time. Toast the bread on both sides, then butter and place on a baking tray. Pour the sauce over the bread and pop it under the grill until bubbling and golden.

Always ask an adult's permission before using kitchen equipment.

Liberty X

Perfect!

This is fantastic! I love being in the saddle.

A Mandy Classic from 1994

*J*ULIE BURCHELL *was mad about horses, and spent every spare moment riding her pony, Pixie.*

Oh! There's Sadie and Amy, with their ponies.

Hi, Julie.

We're going for a canter. Come and join us!

Great!

But —

Hang on! I can't keep up!

Tch! I'll have to let them go. Pixie's old and slow, so fast ponies like Shell and Zee just leave her behind.

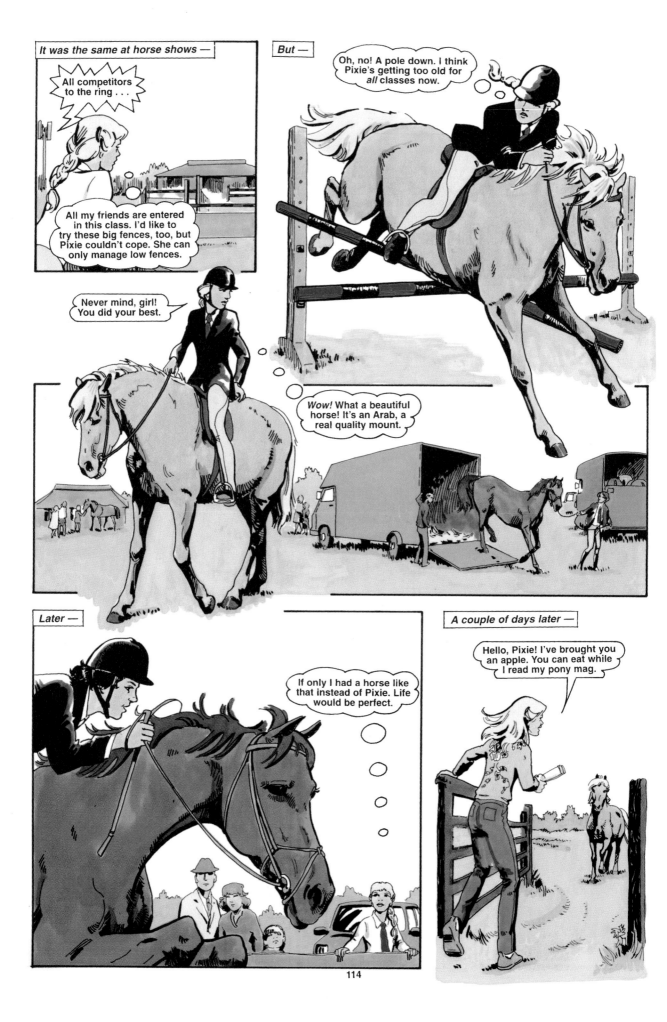

It was the same at horse shows —

All competitors to the ring . . .

All my friends are entered in this class. I'd like to try these big fences, too, but Pixie couldn't cope. She can only manage low fences.

But —

Oh, no! A pole down. I think Pixie's getting too old for *all* classes now.

Never mind, girl! You did your best.

Wow! What a beautiful horse! It's an Arab, a real quality mount.

Later —

If only I had a horse like that instead of Pixie. Life would be perfect.

A couple of days later —

Hello, Pixie! I've brought you an apple. You can eat while I read my pony mag.

Brilliant! Here's a competition to win an Arab horse! I'll definitely enter *this*!

Then, three weeks later —

Letter for you, Julie.

It's very official looking. I wonder what it is.

Oh! It's from my pony mag! *I've won!* I've won the *Arab horse!* Providing I can prove I have a suitable place to keep it, they'll deliver my horse at the end of the week!

But it's expensive keeping *one* horse. We can't afford to pay for food, tack, the vet and blacksmith's fees for *two*.

Then I'll just have to sell Pixie. It's time for me to move on to a better horse. I'll put an ad in the paper.

At the newspaper office —

I'd like to put an ad in the paper. I want to sell my pony.

Have you gone off riding?

No! It's not that. I've won a competition and . . .

When Julie had finished —

That's very interesting! It would make a nice little story, with a photograph as well.

I'll send one of our photographers and a reporter round to see you. Will next week do? We're a bit busy until then.

Sure!

Mum and Dad won't mind me having two horses for a few days. And, once the story's in the paper, I'm sure to sell Pixie quickly. It'll be much better publicity than just an ad.

And, a few days later —

This is your Arab — Desert Prince.

Thank you! He — he's perfect!

Soon —

He goes like the wind, too! My friends will never leave me behind again.

And what a jumper! We'll manage the junior jumping challenge easily next time. Maybe even the *senior* competitions!

You're a beautiful horse, Desert Prince! I'm so lucky to own you.

Oh! He's run off. Pixie always stayed while I chatted to her. Oh, well, all horses are different.

Next morning —

Hello, Pixie! I'm going to make up some more jumps for Desert Prince to try.

He hasn't come to welcome me, like Pixie has.

Then —

Ow! I've dropped a pole on my foot.

He's certainly nothing like Pixie — in *lots* of ways! I wonder . . .

You're a pet, Pixie. You heard me scream and you came to protect me.

Desert Prince hasn't bothered, though. He hardly even glanced over here.

117

puzzle answers

Eyes Down! (page 11)

```
S E L E P H A N T S E C
R U A Y L B G G O D E H
K K M I E I E R D R Z E
H A O A R K E A L A N E
O N N A T C N L R Z A T
R T F G O O A O R I P A
S F A N A M R M D L M H
E V I C A R P O E A I G
A H Y N O P O E R L H O
R E T S M A H O E R C A
C O W M O N K E Y H I T
T I G E R E S U O M S H
```

The hidden word is AARDVARK

It's Christmas!
(pages 22&23)

Scrambled!
HAPPY HOLIDAYS TO ALL
MANDY ANNUAL READERS

The Name Game
a) Carol Smillie b) Santa
c) Rudolph d) Halle Berry (well,
we said it was a bit of a cheat!)

Go Glitter!
Bells; ivy; tree; turkey; bows;
pudding. The hidden word is
tinsel

Hang Around!
Across:
2. Santa 3. Snow 6. Dinner
Down:
1. Gifts 2. Stocking
4. Pantomime 5. Cards

Odd One Out!
Rudolph is b
(He has one short antler)

Puzzling!
Jigsaw

Let's Visit...

France (page 21)
Brittany is not a city, it is
a region.
Quasimodo was the
Hunchback of Notre-
Dame.
'Chateau' is the French
word for castle.

Switzerland (page 42)
The odd one out is
Belladonna. The others
are Swiss cities.
William Tell.
Push him down a hill.
Ha, ha, ha!

Spain (page 72)
Each word appears
twice.
Majorca is the larger
island.
'Adios' means goodbye.

**The British Isles
(page 110)**
Lothian is the odd one
out. It is in Scotland
and the others are in
England.
Northern Ireland.
False - of course!

Work it out!
(pages 78 & 79)

Love or Hate?

```
S C H O O L
C H O C O L A T E
      S L U G S
P A R T I E S
    S P I D E R S
      R A I N
B O Y S
M U S I C
```

The highlighted word
is HOLIDAYS

What Are They?
1. Ring pull 2. Button
3. Pound coin
4. Book 5. Safety pin
6. Mobile phone
7. Spectacles
8. Scissors 9. Watch
10. Fork 11. Key
12. Headphone

What Order?
Wake up
Switch off alarm clock
Get out of bed
Have shower
Get dressed
Go to school

Puzzled? (page 109)

```
T H G I L J C S H O E S C S
D R U E K A M U L O E I U R
N R O D B J J A R R V T S E
N O E S C O M P U T E R H P
I B R S T P R T M V A M I P
G M D N S E C D U H Q I O I
H O R H A X R D R Y E R N L
T C A E P M N S B A N R S S
I D M K Y O E G A R W O R E
E T E P R A C N G R U R I H
Z T C U D D L Y T O Y S A T
C E M U F R E P U S W O H O
F P Y J A M A S D D C N C L
W O L L I P Y C K G O L C C
```

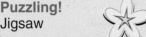

119

I SPY!

'Bye, love. don't forget to wear your scarf when you're outside. It's really cold today.

I won't, Mum . . .

. . . at least, not when you can see me! There's no way I'm wearing this old thing at school.

And the glasses can go, too. I don't want Alan Beadle to see me looking like a dweeb.

But, at school —

So now you can see the answer quite clearly.

Mmm! Not exactly! It's all a bit of a blur, really.

Oh, very funny! I'll see you tomorrow in town, since it's the weekend.

Sure — unless you're in bed with a cold, that is!

I hate my glasses and this stupid scarf! Alan doesn't notice me when I look my best, so there's no way I'd let him see me looking like *this*!

On Saturday morning in town —

Oh, no! It's Alan! And he's with Sarah Summerton! No wonder he's never bothered about me.

What a fool I've been. Fancy imagining Alan could ever be interested in *me*.

I might as well wear these now! At least it'll save me from Nat's nagging!

Don't look now, but Alan's behind us!

m not interested any more, Nat.

Much!

I know I've no chance with Alan, but I still can't get him out of my mind!

It's him. Well, I can be sure that he's not looking for me.

Come on, Gina. Cheer up. No guy is worth all this misery.

You're right, Nat. And I've reached a decision, too.

I'm going to start wearing my glasses from now on.

Great! You should wear your scarf, too! Let's get inside before you freeze!

THE END

125